Ctrl-Alt-CALM

97 Hacks for Busy People on a Budget to Crush Anxiety, Overcome Mental Health Challenges, and Thrive in Chaos

Abiodun Adesina

Ctrl-Alt-CALM
Copyright © 2025, Abiodun A. Adesina
All rights reserved.

This book is under legal protection and only for personal use. You cannot change, distribute, sell, quote, or paraphrase any part of it without permission from the publisher. This book is for educational and entertainment purposes only. We've done our best to make sure the information is correct and complete, but we can't guarantee it's perfect. Readers acknowledge the author is not providing legal, financial, medical, or professional advice. Consult a licensed professional before trying any technique described. By reading this document, you agree the author is not liable for losses, direct or indirect, arising from the use of the information, including but not limited to errors, omissions, or inaccuracies.

For business discussions, contact 752books@3pplea.com.

For questions, concerns, or counseling, please email abiodun.adesina@gmail.com.

Publisher: Absolute Author Publishing House
Editor: Dr. Melissa Caudle

Paperback ISBN: 979-8-89401-068-7

PRINTED IN THE UNITED STATES OF AMERICA

Foreword

Stress is inevitable in today's world. It can manifest because of work, family, or concerns on various levels. As a doctor, politician, and religious leader, I have witnessed the harmful effects of mental health issues.

This book is all about practical, accessible, and affordable solutions for mental health issues. It speaks to the specific pressures faced by working-class individuals and families, making it relatable to everyone.

This guide is a valuable resource for anyone dealing with mental health challenges. Its pages offer not just gains but transformative insights. Engage with an open mind to embrace the suggested changes; your mental well-being is worth it.

Dr. Kehinde Olayiwola Ololade

MBBS (Lag), FWACS, FCNP (SA), MMed (Pret)

About This Book

As your alarm rings, you're already burdened by a stressful day ahead, filled with responsibilities and unfinished tasks.

Our emphasis on being busy makes it easy to overlook the importance of mental health. You should nurture your mind daily, as you would your body. This book is to help you find proven, accessible, and budget-friendly strategies to nurture your mind and mental wellness.

This book provides easy-to-follow strategies. The stories show that mental health is real and can affect anyone, no matter their gender, status, or race.

As you use these insights to achieve your goals, it's a lifelong journey, and this book is your companion. Turn the page and begin your path to a more balanced and fulfilling life.

Acknowledgment

I'm grateful to God for inspiring this book—big thanks to my family for their support and resourcefulness. I want to thank all the experts, leaders, and media teams for their contributions.

Special thanks to Dr. Kehinde Ololade for his time to proofread and write the foreword. He's a leader in medicine, politics, and religion, with experience in stress and mental health.

I thank Dr. Sharon Heller and others for their comments. The feedback helped improve the quality of this book.

This acknowledgment cannot be complete without my special thanks to Dr. Melissa Caudle. She edited and carried out most of the finishing on this book. Dr. Mel (as she's fondly called) is a successful American bestselling author best known for her psychological thriller series "The Keystroke Killer" and "Never Stop Running."

I appreciate everyone's contributions.

Dedication

I'm grateful and honored that you have chosen this book to accompany you on your mental health journey. Your choice shows your courage, resilience, and hope.

I dedicate this book to you—a celebration of your strength and commitment to mental wellness. May every page inspire and empower you to embrace the life you deserve.

Your Free Gift!

"Claim Your Free One-Year PREMIUM Subscription to the Ctrl-Alt-CALM App (Coming Soon!)

Get ready to enhance your mental wellness journey with the Ctrl-Alt-CALM app, a digital companion to our bestselling book! The app is currently in development and expected to launch in Q2, 2025.

As a special thank you for your early support, we're offering a FREE one-year PREMIUM subscription to everyone who purchases the book!

Join our email list to receive exclusive updates on the app's progress and be the first to know when it launches!"

What's Inside:

 ➢ Daily habit & mood tracking

 ➢ Guided mindfulness exercises & Stress Management

 ➢ Budget-friendly wellness tools & resource hub

 ➢ Ctrl-Alt-CALM Mental Health Support Services

 ➢ Validated Mood Scale Integration using PHQ-9 or GAD-7 for accurate self-assessment

 ➢ Community Hub

- Sleep & Energy Optimizer
- AI-Driven Insights/Recommendations
- Wearables Integration
- Participation in selected 5 minutes – 30-day Challenges
- 🎧 5-Minute Stress Resets: Audio guides for traffic jams or meltdowns.
- 🖨 Printable Wins Tracker: Celebrate progress, not perfection.

…. and many more.

Claim It Now by registering your email for the PREMIUM version of the Ctrl-Alt-CALM App.

TABLE OF CONTENTS

CHAPTER ONE: INTRODUCTION 1
   REMEMBER YOUR BEST DAY? 1

CHAPTER TWO: MENTAL HEALTH ON A BUDGET 5
   IT DOESN'T COST A LOT OF MONEY 5

CHAPTER THREE: THE IMPACT OF ROUTINE ON MENTAL HEALTH 10
   ROUTINES ARE ESSENTIAL 10

CHAPTER FOUR: MEDITATION & MINDFUL MOMENTS 15
   MINDFULNESS COMES FROM WITHIN 15

CHAPTER FIVE: PHYSICAL EXERCISE AS A MENTAL HEALTH TOOL 19
   NO GYM REQUIRED 19

CHAPTER SIX: NUTRITION AND MENTAL CLARITY 24
   EAT WELL, THINK CLEAR WITHOUT BREAKING THE BANK 24

CHAPTER SEVEN: CREATIVE STRESS RELIEF ON A BUDGET 28
   UNLEASH CALM THROUGH ART, MUSIC, AND PLAY 28

CHAPTER EIGHT: SLEEP HACKS FOR EXHAUSTED INDIVIDUALS 33
   RECLAIM REST, BOOST MOOD, AND THRIVE WITHOUT EXPENSIVE GADGETS. 33

CHAPTER NINE: DIGITAL DETOX FOR MENTAL CLARITY 38
   RECLAIM FOCUS, REDUCE STRESS, AND RECONNECT WITHOUT QUITTING TECH COLD TURKEY 38

CHAPTER TEN: COMMUNITY & CONNECTION ON A BUDGET 43
   BUILD YOUR SUPPORT SQUAD WITHOUT SPENDING A DIME 43

CHAPTER ELEVEN: BUDGET THERAPY 47
   SIMPLE STEPS TO CRUSH STRESS AND TAKE CONTROL 47

- CHAPTER TWELVE: WORK-LIFE BALANCE WITHOUT BURNOUT 52
  - SIMPLE HACKS TO THRIVE AT WORK AND HOME 52
- CHAPTER THIRTEEN: NATURE THERAPY ON A BUDGET 56
  - FIND CALM IN GREEN SPACES, NO HIKING REQUIRED 56
- CHAPTER FOURTEEN: LAUGHTER & JOY ON A BUDGET 60
  - BOOST MENTAL HEALTH WITH FREE, EVERYDAY DELIGHTS 60
- CHAPTER FIFTEEN: FAMILY DYNAMICS ON A BUDGET 65
  - STRENGTHEN BONDS, BUILD RESILIENCE, AND THRIVE TOGETHER 65
- CHAPTER SIXTEEN: VOLUNTEERISM ON A BUDGET 69
  - BOOST YOUR MOOD BY HELPING OTHERS NO TIME OR MONEY NEEDED 69
- CHAPTER SEVENTEEN: HEALING THROUGH BOOKS 73
  - HOW READING CAN BOOST MENTAL HEALTH, NO COST REQUIRED 73
- CHAPTER EIGHTEEN: MUSIC AS MENTAL MEDICINE 77
  - HARNESS SOUND FOR CALM, JOY, AND CONNECTION 77
- CHAPTER NINETEEN: AFFIRMATIONS ON A BUDGET 81
  - BOOST CONFIDENCE & CRUSH NEGATIVITY, ZERO COST REQUIRED 81
- CHAPTER TWENTY: SPIRITUAL HEALING AND MENTAL HEALTH 85
  - FAITH-BASED TOOLS FOR PEACE, STRENGTH, AND RENEWED PURPOSE 85
- CHAPTER TWENTY-ONE: LONG-TERM PLANNING FOR MENTAL RESILIENCE 90
  - SUSTAIN YOUR PROGRESS WITH VALUES, DRIVEN HABITS & FLEXIBLE STRATEGIES 90
- CHAPTER TWENTY-TWO: CONCLUSION 96
  - YOUR JOURNEY TO LIFELONG MENTAL WELLNESS STARTS NOW 96
- ABOUT THE AUTHOR 101
- REFERENCES 104
- INDEX 105

Chapter One

Introduction

Remember Your Best Day?

Have you ever had a day when everything just clicked? Maybe you laughed with friends, aced a project, or felt completely at ease. That feeling of balance and calm—that's good mental health at work. But what happens when stress, anxiety, or burnout throw that balance off?

Did you know that nearly one in five adults in the U.S. lives with a mental illness? In today's whirlwind of work, family, and endless to-dos, it's easy to feel overwhelmed. We're constantly told to "hustle harder," but what about taking care of our minds? This book is your guide to finding balance and calm, even when life feels chaotic.

Why This Book

Affordable Solutions: Proven strategies that won't break the bank.

Time-Saving Hacks: Quick and easy tips that fit into your daily routine.

Science-Backed & Practical: simple, actionable steps based on research.

This book isn't just about theory; it's a hands-on guide designed for busy people like you. Whether you're a working professional, a parent juggling responsibilities, or a student trying to manage stress, the goal is simple: help you achieve better mental health without spending a fortune.

Let's get started—your journey to better mental wellness begins now.

Your Invisible Backpack

Think of mental health as a backpack you carry everywhere. Inside are your:

- Thoughts ("Can I handle this?")
- Emotions (joy, fear, anger)
- Resilience (how you bounce back)

This backpack affects everything: how you work, love, and make decisions. Ignore it, and the weight drags you down. Tend to it, and you'll walk taller.

Meet Sarah: A Day in the Life of Burnout

Sarah, a single mom of two, juggles two jobs. Her daily struggles mirror what millions face:

5:00 AM: Up before dawn. Rush kids to school.

8:00 AM: Anxious commute. Heart races thinking about bills.

Work: Endless emails. Coworkers chat about weekends; she feels alone.

5:30 PM: Kids forgot homework again. Guilt hits: "I'm failing as a mom."

10:00 PM: Exhausted but can't sleep. Hobbies? No energy.

Sarah's Backpack Is Overflowing:

- ✓ Constant worry
- ✓ Isolation
- ✓ Lost joy

Sound familiar?

Why Mental Health Matters for Busy Lives

- Seventy percent of working adults say job stress harms their mental health (APA).
- 1 in 3 employees' performance suffers due to depression.
- Depression and anxiety are the top causes of disability worldwide (WHO).

The Domino Effect: Poor mental health raises risks for heart disease, diabetes, and more.

Good News: Small Changes = Big Shifts

You don't need expensive therapy or a month-long retreat. This book is your toolbox for:

- **Quick Fixes:** 5-minute hacks to calm anxiety.
- **Family Wins:** Bonding activities that cost $0.
- **Community Support:** Two or more are better than one.
- **Work-Life Resets:** Prioritize without guilt.

Example: A busy nurse reduced burnout by journaling three gratitudes daily. You can, too.

What's Ahead

Part 1: Understand anxiety, depression, burnout, and other mental health issues (no jargon!).

Part 2: 90+ budget-friendly hacks for individuals & families.

Part 3: Build a support system—no therapist required.

Your First Step

Ask yourself: "What's one small thing I can do to lighten my backpack?"

Chapter Two

Mental Health on a Budget

It Doesn't Cost a lot of Money

Mental health is essential to overall well-being, influencing how we think, feel, and navigate life's challenges. It affects our relationships, decision-making, and ability to cope with stress, making it just as important as physical health. When mental health is prioritized, individuals are better equipped to handle adversity, maintain healthy connections, and pursue personal and professional goals with clarity and confidence. Neglecting mental health can lead to emotional distress, decreased productivity, and even physical health issues.

By fostering self-care, seeking support when needed, and promoting mental wellness, we create a foundation for a balanced, fulfilling life. Prioritizing mental health is not just about managing difficulties—it's about thriving.

Why Mental Health Care Feels Out of Reach

Mental healthcare can be expensive. In the U.S., therapy sessions cost anywhere from $100–$250 per hour, while in lower-income countries, mental health professionals are scarce—often fewer than one per 100,000 people (APA, 2023).

Costs in High-Income Countries:

Therapy: $100–250 per session.

Treatment programs: $500–2,000/day.

Community clinics/NGOs: $0–50/session.

Low-Income Countries:

Fewer than one mental health professional per 100,000 people.

Most can't access care.

You're Not Alone.

Seventy percent of working adults say stress harms their mental health (APA). Expensive or unavailable services compound this challenge.

Good news: This book is your guide to affordable solutions, as good mental health doesn't have to cost a fortune.

Top 5 Mental Health Challenges (And How to Spot Them)

Anxiety

Anxiety is more than just feeling worried. It can involve racing thoughts, a pounding heart, restlessness, and difficulty concentrating. It's important to distinguish between everyday anxiety and an anxiety disorder, which is more persistent and interferes with daily life. Anxiety disorders are the most common mental health concern in the U.S. and the world over, affecting millions of adults.

It feels like a racing heart, overthinking, and restlessness.

Budget Fix: Try the 4-7-8 breathing technique—inhale for 4 seconds, hold for 7, exhale for 8.

Depression

It's a persistent feeling of sadness, hopelessness, and loss of interest in things you once enjoyed. It can also involve fatigue, changes in appetite, and difficulty sleeping. Depression can make it hard to get out of bed in the morning, let alone face the day.

It feels like no motivation, constant fatigue, and loss of joy.

Budget Fix: 10-minute walks in natural sunlight—proven to boost mood by increasing serotonin (Harvard Study, 2021).

Burnout

Burnout is a state of emotional, physical, and mental exhaustion caused by prolonged or excessive stress. It can lead to feelings of cynicism, detachment, and reduced performance. Burnout can make you feel like you're running on empty, with no energy left to give.

It feels like exhaustion, detachment, lack of motivation.

Budget Fix: Set "no-work" hours and stick to them—balance is key.

PTSD (Post-Traumatic Stress Disorder)

PTSD can develop after experiencing or witnessing a traumatic event. Symptoms can include flashbacks, nightmares, anxiety, and avoidance of triggers. PTSD can make it feel like you're reliving the trauma over and over again. It is triggered by trauma, loss, and abuse.

Budget Fix: Join free online support groups—community is healing.

Loneliness & Isolation

Feeling disconnected from others can have a significant impact on mental health. Loneliness and isolation can increase the risk of depression, anxiety, and other health problems. We are social creatures, and we need the connection to thrive.

It feels like disconnection, sadness, social anxiety.

Budget Fix: Send a "thinking of you" text to a friend—human connection matters.

The Global Cost of Ignoring Mental Health

- $6 trillion: What poor mental health will cost the economy by 2030 (WEF).
- 1 in 7 teens has a mental health condition (WHO).
- 10–20 years shorter life for those with severe mental illness.

Your Power Move: Start small. Even 5 minutes of self-care daily adds up.

4 Free Ways to Boost Mental Health TODAY

- Walk & Breathe: No gym? Stroll around your block. Inhale for 4 counts, exhale for 6.
- Recycle Old Hobbies: Dust off that guitar or sketchbook—creativity reduces stress.
- Screen Time Swap: Replace 15 minutes of scrolling with a funny podcast.
- Talk to a Plant: Sounds silly? Verbalizing worries helps—even to a fern!

Tech Tools on a Budget

- Ctrl-Alt-CALM: Free version for guided meditation.
- Moodfit: Track moods + spot triggers (no cost).
- YouTube: Search "5-minute yoga for anxiety."
- Pro Tip: Use public Wi-Fi to download apps if data is tight.

Your Action Plan

- Pick One Hack: Try a 5-minute walk or breathing exercise today.
- Find One Resource: Google "[Your town] + free mental health workshop."
- Share One Tip: Text this chapter to a friend who's struggling.

Next Up: Chapter 3 dives into the Impact of Routine on Mental Health.

Chapter Three

The Impact of Routine on Mental Health

Routines are Essential

Routines are structured, consistent habits or behaviors that help bring order and stability to daily life. They provide a sense of predictability, making it easier to manage time, reduce stress, and improve overall productivity.

Routines are important because they create a foundation for physical and mental well-being, helping individuals establish healthy habits such as regular exercise, proper sleep, and balanced nutrition.

They also enhance focus and efficiency by reducing decision fatigue, allowing people to dedicate more energy to meaningful tasks. Whether for work, self-care, or relaxation, routines foster discipline, build resilience, and contribute to long-term success and happiness.

Why Routines Matter

Routines aren't about rigid schedules—they're your secret weapon to fight stress and feel in control. Studies show routines slash anxiety by 40% and boost focus. But how do you start?

The Magic Formula:

- Small steps > Overhauling your life.
- Flexibility > Perfection.

Small steps at a time are more effective than a one-time overhaul; Flexibility is more effective than perfection, etc.

Top 9 Routine Challenges (and How to Beat Them)

"I'm too busy!"

Fix: Start with ONE 5-minute habit (e.g., deep breathing while brushing your teeth).

"I keep procrastinating."

Fix: Pair new habits with existing ones (e.g., stretch after your morning coffee).

"I hate feeling trapped."

Fix: Build "flex blocks" into your day. No guilt if plans change!

"I'm bored."

Fix: Swap routines weekly—try yoga on Monday and dance breaks on Tuesday.

"I forget!"

Fix: Set phone alarms labeled "BREATHE" or "WALK."

"I'm too tired at night."

Fix: Prep tomorrow's to-do list in 2 minutes before bed.

"I can't stick to it."

Fix: Track progress with a sticky note checklist or free apps—no costly apps needed.

"Work drains me."

Fix: Use the Pomodoro Technique: Work 25 mins, break 5 mins.

"My family resists."

Fix: Turn routines into games, e.g., "Who can drink the most water today?"

Morning & Evening Rituals Made Simple

For Busy Mornings:

- 5-Minute Jumpstart:
- Stretch like a cat (2 mins).
- Write one thing you're grateful for (1 min).
- Eat a banana (2 mins)—no cooking required!

For Peaceful Nights:

- Screen-Free Zone: Ditch devices 1 hour before bed. Try:
- Reading a paperback (even 1 chapter!).
- Sipping caffeine-free tea.

Real-Life Win: Sarah, a single mom, added 10-minute walks during her kids' soccer practice. "It's my sanity saver!"

Workplace Hacks (No Boss Approval Needed)

- Mindful Lunches: Eat away from your desk. Taste each bite—no emails!
- Gratitude Jar: Jot one win per day on a sticky note. Read them on Fridays.
- Desk Yoga: Try seated twists or shoulder rolls hourly.

Did You Know? A financial firm cut stress by 32% by adding 5-minute mindfulness breaks.

Habit Tracking for Busy People

Free Tools to Try:

Ctrl-Alt-CALM App.

Habitica: Turn routines into a game (unlock dragons for brushing teeth!).

Pen & Paper: Draw a weekly chart. Add stickers for wins—kids love this!

Pro Tip: Pair up! Text a friend: "Did you walk today?" (Like Lisa and Tom, coworkers who kept each other on track.)

When to Tweak Your Routine

Ask weekly: "Is this habit helping or stressing me?"

Example: Emily swapped rigid gym sessions for lunchtime walks. Result? Less burnout, more joy.

Your Action Plan

Pick One Tiny Habit: Start tomorrow (e.g., 5-minute stretch).

- Celebrate Small Wins: High-five yourself for sticking to it!
- Share the Load: Involve your family—make routines a team effort.

Up Next: Meditation & Mindful Moments.

Chapter Four

Meditation & Mindful Moments

Mindfulness Comes from Within

Mindfulness is the practice of being fully present in the moment and aware of thoughts, emotions, and surroundings without judgment. It involves consciously focusing on the here and now rather than dwelling on the past or worrying about the future. Meditation is a powerful tool that connects to mindfulness by training the mind to stay centered and calm, fostering a sense of inner peace and clarity.

Through meditation, individuals can cultivate greater self-awareness, emotional regulation, and stress management, all of which contribute to better mental health. Regular mindfulness and meditation practices have been shown to reduce anxiety, improve focus, and enhance overall well-being.

By integrating these practices into daily life, individuals can build resilience, develop a more positive mindset, and create a deeper sense of balance and tranquility.

Why Mindfulness Matters (Even When Life's Crazy)

Mindfulness isn't about sitting cross-legged for hours—it's noticing your thoughts without judgment. Think of it as a "pause button" for stress.

Science Says: Just 5 minutes daily can lower anxiety by 30% (APA).

Quick Hacks to Find Calm in Chaos

5-Minute Breathing Hack: The 4-Count Breath

No apps, no mats, no fuss.

How to Do It:

Breathe In (nose, 4 seconds).

Hold (4 seconds).

Breathe Out (mouth, 4 seconds).

Repeat 3x.

Where to Try It:

At your desk.

In traffic.

While microwaving leftovers.

Bonus: Add a mantra: "Inhale calm, exhale chaos."

Mindful Eating for Busy Lives

Turn meals into mini meditations.

3 Steps to Try Tonight:

- Check Your Hunger: Ask, "Am I eating from stress or hunger?"
- Slow Down: Chew 10 times per bite. Taste the flavors!
- Ditch Screens: No phones/TV. Just you and your plate.

Pro Tip: Use colorful plates—it tricks your brain into savoring meals more.

Real People, Real Results

Sarah (Busy Mom):

Challenge: Anxiety from non-stop work and demand for kids' care.

Fix: 5-minute morning breathing + gratitude journal.

Result: "I yell less, laugh more."

James (Emotional Eater):

Challenge: Stress snacking.

Fix: Ate one snack mindfully daily (no distractions).

Result: Lost 15 lbs. and sleep better.

Lina (Burnt-Out Teacher):

Challenge: Classroom stress.

Fix: 2-minute desk stretches between classes.

Result: "My students are calmer because I'm calmer."

Your Action Plan

- Try the 4-Count breath today (set a phone reminder!).
- Pick one meal to eat mindfully this week.
- Share a Win: Text a friend, "I breathed through chaos today!"

Need Help?

Free Apps

Ctrl-Alt-CALM, Smiling Mind (no cost).

YouTube Search: "3-minute meditation for work stress."

Next Up: Chapter 5 - Physical Exercise as a Mental Health Tool.

Chapter Five

Physical Exercise as a Mental Health Tool

No Gym Required

Physical exercise is a powerful tool for improving mental health, as it helps reduce stress, anxiety, and depression while boosting overall well-being. Engaging in regular physical activity releases endorphins—often called "feel-good" hormones—that enhance mood and promote relaxation. Exercise also improves sleep, increases energy levels, and strengthens cognitive function, making it easier to manage daily challenges.

Whether through walking, yoga, strength training, or sports, movement provides an outlet for stress relief and emotional regulation. Additionally, staying active fosters self-discipline, builds confidence, and encourages a positive mindset.

By making physical exercise a consistent part of life, individuals can support both their mental and physical health, creating a foundation for long-term wellness.

Why Exercise is Your Brain's Best Friend

Did You Know?

Just 10 minutes of exercise can zap stress and boost happiness.

Science Says:

- Cuts anxiety by 48% (ADAA).
- Reduces depression risk by 30% (WHO).
- Boosts sleep quality by 40% (CDC).

How It Works: Exercise releases endorphins (your brain's "feel-good" chemicals) and helps you sleep better. Think of it as a free antidepressant!

Home Workouts on a Budget

No equipment? No problem! Try these anytime, anywhere:

1. Stairway to Zen:

Walk up and down stairs for 5 mins.

Bonus: Pretend you're climbing a mountain!

2. Chair Power:

Sit-to-stands (10 reps).

Leg lifts while brushing teeth.

3. Laundry Day Lunges:

Lunge toward the laundry basket (10x per side).

4. Dance Breaks:

Blast a favorite song and shake it out for 3 minutes.

Pro Tip: Use canned goods as weights or a towel as a yoga mat.

5-Minute Mood Boosters

For busy days:

- Sun Salute: Stretch arms up, touch toes, repeat (2 mins).
- Jumping Jacks: 1 minute (or march in place if joints ache).
- Deep Breathing: 2 mins (inhale calm, exhale stress).
- Real-Life Win: Emma, a mom of three, does squats while cooking pasta. "It keeps my anxiety in check!"

Family Fitness Fun

Bond and move together:

Living Room Olympics: Timed races, pillow fights, or yoga poses.

Nature Scavenger Hunts: Walk while spotting birds, flowers, or clouds.

Dance-Off Fridays: Turn chores into dance parties.

Budget Hack: Use free YouTube workouts (search "family Zumba" or "kids yoga").

Track Progress Without Apps

Keep it simple:

- Mood & Movement Journal:
- Monday: 10-min walk → Felt energized.
- Wednesday: Dance break → Laughed with kids.

- Sticker Chart: Kids earn stickers for every active day.

Match Exercise to Your Mood

Stressed? Try yoga or slow stretching.

Angry? Punch a pillow (safely!) or try kickboxing moves.

Sad? Walk outside—sunlight boosts serotonin.

Pro Tip: Hate running? Swap it for gardening, walking the dog, or playing tag.

Join the Movement (For Free!)

- Community Walks: Check local parks or schools for groups.
- Online Challenges: #30DayFitness on Instagram.
- Library Classes: Many offer free tai chi or aerobics.

Real-Life Wins

Sarah's Story:

Challenge: Anxiety about work deadlines.

Fix: 10-minute morning yoga + lunchtime walks.

Result: "I'm calmer and sleep like a baby!"

Michael Phelps' Tip:

"Swimming saved me. Find your movement—even if it's just stretching!"

Your Action Plan

- Start Small: Pick one 5-minute workout (try the stairs!).

- Rally the Troops: Text your family, "Who's up for a dance-off tonight?"
- Celebrate: High-five yourself after each session—progress, not perfection!

Up Next: Chapter 6 - Nutrition and Mental Clarity.

Chapter Six

Nutrition and Mental Clarity

Eat Well, Think Clear Without Breaking the Bank

Food is the brain's fuel, providing the essential nutrients needed for cognitive function, mood regulation, and overall mental well-being. Just like the body, the brain requires a balanced diet rich in vitamins, minerals, healthy fats, and proteins to function at its best. Nutrient-dense foods, such as fruits, vegetables, whole grains, and omega-3 fatty acids, support memory, focus, and emotional stability, while processed foods and excess sugar can contribute to brain fog, fatigue, and mood swings.

Proper nutrition also plays a role in reducing the risk of mental health disorders like depression and anxiety. By fueling the brain with wholesome, nourishing foods, individuals can enhance their mental clarity, boost energy levels, and maintain a healthier, more resilient mind.

Why Food is Your Brain's Fuel

Ever feel foggy after a fast-food meal or sharp after a salad? What you eat directly impacts focus, mood, and energy.

Science confirms:

- Diets rich in fruits, veggies, and healthy fats boost memory and cut anxiety.
- Processed foods? They're linked to brain fog and mood swings.

Good news: You don't need expensive superfoods. Let's hack your diet for mental clarity!

Top 5 Budget Brain Foods

Frozen Blueberries

Why: Packed with antioxidants.

Save: Cheaper than fresh, just as healthy.

Eat: Toss in oatmeal or blend into smoothies.

Canned Sardines

Why: Packed with omega-3s (critical for brain health).

Save: Stretch 1 tin into 2–3 servings (e.g., 2 meals for one or split across family dishes).

Eat: Mash onto whole-grain toast for a 5-minute snack, or stir into pasta for an easy, nutrient-dense dinner.

Oats

Why: Steady energy, no crash.

Save: Buy in bulk for pennies per meal.

Eat: Overnight oats with peanut butter + banana.

Eggs

Why: Choline for memory, protein for focus.

Save: Costs as low as $0.15–0.25 per egg when bought in bulk.

Eat: Scramble with spinach for a 5-minute breakfast.

Carrots + Hummus

Why: Fiber + healthy fats = happy gut, happy brain.

Save: Pre-cut veggies cost more—chop your own!

Meal Prep Hacks for Busy Families

Batch-Cook Sundays: Make a giant pot of veggie soup or chili (freeze leftovers).

Theme Nights:

- Taco Tuesday: Whole-grain tortillas + beans + salsa.
- Stir-Fry Friday: Frozen veggies + rice + soy sauce.
- Kid-Friendly DIY Bars: Let kids build their own plates (e.g., "bowl night" with grains, veggies, and proteins).

Pro Tip: Use a muffin tin for portioned snacks—nuts, berries, cheese cubes.

Fix Your Mood with Food

Feeling anxious? Try magnesium-rich foods: spinach, almonds, dark chocolate (70%+).

Sluggish? Swap sugary snacks for apple slices + almond butter.

Stressed? Sip chamomile tea—it's cheaper than lattes!

Real-Life Win: Maria, a single mom, swapped soda for infused water (lemon + mint). "My kids focus better, and I'm less irritable!"

Gut-Brain Connection Made Simple

Your gut and brain chat non-stop. Keep them happy with:

Probiotics: Yogurt, sauerkraut, or kimchi (cheap at local markets).

Fiber: Beans, oats, and bananas feed good gut bugs.

Avoid: Too much sugar—it fuels bad bacteria and brain fog.

Your Action Plan

- Pick One Brain Food: Add it to your next grocery list.
- Try a 5-Minute Meal: Scrambled eggs + frozen spinach.
- Hydrate Smart: Ditch soda—infuse water with fruit/herbs.

Need Help?

Free Apps

Mealtime (budget recipes), Too Good To Go (discounted groceries).

YouTube: Search "$5 mental health meals."

Next Up: Chapter 7 - Creative Stress Relief on a Budget.

Chapter Seven

Creative Stress Relief on a Budget

Unleash Calm Through Art, Music, and Play

Creative stress relief is an affordable and effective way to unwind, express emotions, and cultivate inner peace—no talent is required! Engaging in activities like painting, doodling, journaling, or crafting allows the mind to focus on the present moment, reducing anxiety and promoting relaxation.

Music is another powerful stress reliever; simply listening to soothing tunes, singing, or drumming on a table can lift your mood. Playful activities such as dancing, solving puzzles, or engaging in imaginative storytelling also stimulate joy and creativity, helping to release tension.

Best of all, these activities don't require expensive supplies—just a willingness to explore and enjoy the process. By embracing creativity as a form of stress relief, you can nurture your mental well-being while having fun, all without breaking the bank.

Why Creativity Beats Stress

Creativity isn't about skill—it's about letting your emotions flow.

Science says:

- Art reduces anxiety by 30% (NIH).
- Dancing releases "happy chemicals" (endorphins) in 10 minutes.
- Journaling cuts stress by 38% (APA).

Good news: You don't need fancy supplies or hours of free time.

Art Therapy Hacks for Busy Lives

No Picasso skills needed! Try these quick fixes:

1. Doodle Your Stress Away

Supplies: Pen + scrap paper.

How: Scribble shapes or patterns for 5 mins. Focus on the motion, not the result.

2. Vision Board Collage

Supplies: Old magazines, glue, cardboard.

How: Cut out images that make you happy. Glue them together—no rules!

3. Coloring for Grown-Ups

Free Printable: Search "free mindfulness coloring pages."

Pro Tip: Use crayons during kids' nap time.

Family Fun: Host a "Crafternoon"—turn junk mail into collages!

Dance & Music: Move Your Mood

5-Minute Mood Boosters:

- Kitchen Dance Party: Blast a favorite song while cooking.
- Chair Dancing: Shake out stress during work calls (mute your mic!).

Calm Moves:

Stretch & Breathe: Reach up, exhale slowly. Repeat 5x.

Youtube Yoga: Search "5-minute desk yoga."

Real-Life Win: Emily and Tom reconnected with salsa nights. "Laughter is our best therapy!"

Journaling Without Pressure

Start Small: Answer one prompt daily:

"Today, I'm proud of…"

"I felt [emotion] when…"

"One thing I'd let go of…"

Creative Twist: Add stickers or doodles to entries. Kids love this, too!

Free App

Day One (syncs across devices for on-the-go journaling).

Another Successful Outcome

Sarah (Busy Mom):

Challenge: Overwhelmed by parenting + work.

Fix: Daily 20-minute painting sessions during naps.

Result: "My art reminds me I'm more than a to-do list."

Robert (Stressed Accountant):

Challenge: Burnout from spreadsheets.

Fix: Joined a community choir.

Result: "Singing feels like hitting a mental reset button."

Lisa's Family Game Night:

Challenge: No time to bond.

Fix: Themed game nights (puzzles, charades).

Result: "We laugh more, argue less."

Play for Adults. Remember, play isn't just for kids! Engaging in playful activities can help adults reduce stress, boost creativity, and improve relationships. Try:

- Playing board games or card games.
- Building with LEGOs or other construction toys.
- Spending time in nature.
- Engaging in hobbies that bring you joy.

Mindful Creativity. When engaging in creative activities, try to be present in the moment. Focus on the sensory experience—the colors, textures, sounds, and smells—

rather than the end product. Let go of self-judgment and simply enjoy the process.

Your Action Plan

- Try One Hack Today: Doodle, dance, or journal for 5 minutes.
- Involve Your Crew: Turn chores into dance-offs or collages.
- Celebrate Imperfection: Messy art = healthy stress relief!

Need Ideas?

YouTube: Search "10-minute DIY stress toys."

Local Library: Free art workshops or music clubs.

Next Up: Chapter 8 - Sleep Hacks for Exhausted Individuals.

Chapter Eight

Sleep Hacks for Exhausted Individuals

Reclaim Rest, Boost Mood, and Thrive Without Expensive Gadgets

Sleep is essential for overall health and well-being, playing a crucial role in both physical and mental functioning. Quality sleep allows the body to repair itself, supports immune function, and helps regulate hormones that affect mood, stress, and energy levels. It is also vital for brain health, improving memory, concentration, and problem-solving skills.

Without adequate rest, individuals may experience increased irritability, difficulty focusing, and a higher risk of anxiety and depression.

Chronic sleep deprivation can also contribute to serious health issues, such as heart disease and weakened immunity. Prioritizing restful sleep through a consistent bedtime routine, relaxation techniques, and a comfortable sleep environment ensures the mind and body function optimally, leading to better overall well-being.

Myth vs. Fact: Why Sleep Matters

Myth: "I'll sleep when I'm dead."

Fact: Poor sleep tanks your mood, focus, and patience. It's linked to anxiety, weight gain, and even heart issues.

Science Says:

- Just 1 night of bad sleep raises stress hormones by 37% (APA).
- 7–9 hours nightly slashes depression risk by 22% (NIH).

Good News: You don't need a perfect routine, just smarter habits.

6 Budget Hacks for Better Sleep

According to the National Institute of Mental Health (2023), poor sleep increases the risk of anxiety and depression by 40%. The good news? Simple, budget-friendly fixes can drastically improve sleep quality.

Blackout on a Dime

Use aluminum foil or $5 blackout curtains to block light.

Pro Tip: Tape cardboard to windows if noise/light is extreme.

White Noise for Free:

Play "rain sounds" on YouTube or use a fan.

Family Hack: Kids love "ocean wave" apps for bedtime.

Cool It Down:

Ideal sleep temp: 60–67°F.

Cheap Fix: Freeze a washcloth, place it on your neck for 5 mins before bed.

Repurpose Your Pillow:

Stomach sleeper? Hug a pillow to ease back strain.

Side sleeper? Place one between your knees.

Ditch Screens:

Blue light disrupts sleep. Try "screen sundown" 1 hour before bed.

Swap: Read a paperback or do crossword puzzles.

Try the Military Sleep Trick:

Relax each body part from head to toe, imagining yourself sinking into the bed.

5-Minute Fixes for Insomnia

Worry Dump: Write down racing thoughts in a $1 notebook. Close it and say, "I'll handle this tomorrow."

4-7-8 Breath: Inhale 4 secs, hold 7, exhale 8. Repeat 3x.

Military Sleep Trick: Relax each body part head-to-toe, imagining sinking into the bed.

Real-Life Win: Sarah, a student, swapped late-night scrolling for herbal tea + journaling. "I fall asleep 20 minutes faster!"

Family-Friendly Sleep Wins

Bedtime "Power Down" Ritual:

- Dim lights, play soft music, and share "3 good things" about the day.
- Kid Calm-Down Jar:
- Fill a jar with water + glitter. Shake and watch it[settle visual cue to unwind.

Teen Tech Curfew

Charge phones outside bedrooms. Use old-school alarms instead.

Garcia Family's Success:

Challenge: Kids' late-night screen battles.

Fix: "No screens after 8:00 PM" + family storytime.

Result: Less morning chaos, happier moods.

When to Seek Help

Red Flags:

- Snoring loudly or gasping awake.
- Daytime exhaustion for over 2 weeks.
- Mood swings affecting relationships.

Budget Resources:

Free Sleep Clinics: Check local hospitals or universities.

Online CBT-I: Apps like Sleepio offer low-cost insomnia therapy.

Your Action Plan

- Pick One Hack Tonight: Try blackout curtains or the 4-7-8 breath.
- Family Pact: Agree on a "tech curfew" with your kids.
- Track Wins: Use a free app like Sleep Cycle to spot patterns.

Need More?

YouTube: Search "10-minute yoga for sleep."

Library: Borrow Why We Sleep by Matthew Walker.

Next Up: Chapter 9 dives into Digital Detox for Mental Clarity.

Chapter Nine

Digital Detox for Mental Clarity

Reclaim Focus, Reduce Stress, and Reconnect Without Quitting Tech Cold Turkey

In today's hyper-connected world, we are constantly bombarded with notifications, emails, social media updates, and endless streams of digital content. While technology offers convenience and connectivity, it can also lead to mental fatigue, stress, and decreased focus. A **digital detox**—taking intentional breaks from screens—can be a powerful way to restore mental clarity, improve well-being, and regain control over our time and attention.

The Tech Trap: Why It Drains You

Ever scroll through your phone aimlessly, then realize 30 minutes vanished? You're not alone. Constant notifications and screen time:

- Zap focus: Switching tasks drops productivity by 40% (University of Michigan).

- Fuel anxiety: Heavy social media users are 53% more likely to feel lonely (APA).
- Steal sleep: Blue light from screens delays melatonin, keeping you awake.

Good news: Small tweaks can help you use tech without letting it rule your life.

7 Budget Hacks to Set Digital Boundaries

Tech-Free Zones

- Ban phones/tablets from the dinner table and bedrooms.

Family Tip: Use a "phone basket" during meals—whoever grabs theirs first does dishes!

Do Not Disturb Hours:

Block notifications 1 hour before bed + during family time.

Work Hack: Use apps like Freedom or Focus@Will to block distracting sites.

Screen Time Audits:

Check your phone's built-in tracker (e.g., iPhone's Screen Time or Android's Digital Well-being).

Action: Delete one app that wastes your time (looking at you, TikTok!).

The 20-20-20 Rule:

Every 20 minutes, look at something 20 feet away for 20 seconds. Saves eyes and sanity.

Weekend Detox Challenge

Pick four hours each weekend to unplug. Replace scrolling with walks, reading, or baking.

Social Media and Mental Health

Social media can be a double-edged sword. While it can be a way to connect with others, it can also lead to social comparison, cyberbullying, and fear of missing out (FOMO). Be mindful of how social media makes you feel. If you find yourself feeling anxious or depressed after spending time on social media, consider taking a break or limiting your use.

Mindful Tech Use: Technology can be a powerful tool for good. Instead of just focusing on reducing screen time, consider how you can use technology in a way that is positive and beneficial for your mental health. For example:

- Use meditation apps to practice mindfulness.
- Connect with loved ones through video calls.
- Listen to uplifting podcasts or audiobooks.
- Learn new skills through online courses.

Real-Life Wins

Sophia's Social Media Break:

Challenge: Anxiety from comparing herself online.

Fix: Deleted Instagram for 30 days and picked up painting.

Result: "I stopped caring about likes and found my joy again."

The Johnson Family Cabin Trip:

Challenge: Constant screen fights with kids.

Fix: Weekend getaway with no Wi-Fi—just hiking and board games.

Result: "We talked more and laughed louder."

Mark's Mindful Retreat:

Challenge: Burnout from 24/7 emails.

Fix: 3-day tech-free retreat (yoga + journaling).

Result: "I now check emails twice a day, not 50 times."

Family-Friendly Detox Idea

- Screen-Free Sundays: Replace TV with a DIY project (e.g., build a birdhouse).
- Photo Scavenger Hunts: Use a disposable camera to capture fun moments—no filters!
- Cooking Challenges: Whip up meals using recipe books, not YouTube.

Your Action Plan

- Start Small: Turn off notifications for 1 app today.
- Tech-Free Hour: Tonight, replace screens with a walk or puzzle.
- Track Wins: Use a free app like Moment to celebrate progress.

Need Help?

Free Tools

Forest app (grow virtual trees while staying focused).

YouTube: Search "5-minute digital detox yoga."

Next Up: Chapter 10 - Community & Connection on a Budget.

Chapter Ten

Community & Connection on a Budget

Build Your Support Squad Without Spending a Dime

Community and connection refer to the relationships and sense of belonging that individuals share with others, whether through family, friendships, social groups, or local communities.

Having a strong support network is essential for emotional well-being, as it provides comfort, encouragement, and a sense of security during both good and challenging times.

Meaningful connections help reduce feelings of loneliness, boost self-esteem, and promote a sense of purpose. Being part of a community also fosters collaboration, shared experiences, and personal growth, reminding individuals that they are not alone in their journey. Prioritizing relationships and building genuine connections contribute to a happier, healthier, and more fulfilling life.

Why Community Matters

Humans are wired to connect.

Science proves:

- Strong social ties cut depression risk by 50% (Harvard Study).
- Feeling lonely? Just 10 minutes of chatting boosts mood (APA).

Good news: You don't need expensive outings or therapy—meaningful connections are free!

5 Free Ways to Build Your Support Squad

- Host a Potluck: Ask friends to bring leftovers. Focus on laughs, not gourmet meals.
- Join a Walking Group: Meet neighbors for sunrise strolls (exercise + bonding!).
- Start a Skill Swap: Trade guitar lessons for babysitting or garden help.
- Volunteer Together: Food banks, parks, or animal shelters—helping others = instant joy.
- Text a "Check-In" Chain: Message 3 friends: "How are you really?" Pass it on!

Affordable Group Activities

Fun ideas for families and busy folks:

- Park Picnics 👜 : Blanket + sandwiches + frisbee = instant fun.
- DIY Game Nights 🎲 : Dig out old board games or play charades.

- Community Gardens 🌱: Grow veggies and friendships (no green thumb needed).
- Library Clubs 📖: Free book clubs, crafting workshops, or movie nights.

Real-Life Wins

Maria's Book Club:

Challenge: Lonely stay-at-home mom.

Fix: Started a monthly book club at her kitchen table.

Result: "We talk books, then life. I've found my tribe!"

Ben's Anxiety Group:

Challenge: Panic attacks isolated him.

Fix: Joined a free support group at the library.

Result: "Hearing others' stories made me feel less broken."

The Lee Family's Garden:

Challenge: New town, no friends.

Fix: Joined a community garden.

Result: "We grow zucchinis and inside jokes with neighbors!"

Your Action Plan

- Pick One Idea: Host a potluck or join a free walking group this week.
- Say "Yes": Accept invites to local events (even if you're nervous!).

- Be the Connector: Text 2 friends: "Let's [activity] this weekend!"

Need Help?

Apps

Ctrl-Alt-CALM, Meetup (find free local groups) or Nextdoor (connect with neighbors).

Libraries: Ask about free workshops or clubs.

Next Up: Chapter 11 - Budget Therapy Alternatives When Money's Tight.

Chapter Eleven

Budget Therapy

Simple Steps to Crush Stress and Take Control

Money problems are one of the most common sources of stress, impacting mental and emotional well-being in significant ways. Financial struggles can lead to anxiety, depression, and even physical health issues as individuals worry about paying bills, managing debt, or securing their future.

The uncertainty of financial instability can create constant pressure, affecting sleep, relationships, and overall quality of life. Chronic stress caused by money issues may also lead to unhealthy coping mechanisms, such as overeating, substance use, or withdrawing from social connections.

However, addressing financial stress through budgeting, seeking financial guidance, and setting realistic financial goals can help regain a sense of control and reduce anxiety. While money can be a stressful topic, proactive planning and support can lead to financial stability and greater peace of mind.

Why Money Stress Hurts Your Mind

Seventy percent of people say finances are their #1 stressor (APA).

Good news: Small, consistent steps can build confidence and calm.

Build a Budget That Works for You

Step 1: Track Your Cash

Income: List all money coming in (salary, side gigs, gifts).

Expenses: Write down every dollar spent (yes, even that latte).

Step 2: Sort Spending

Needs: Rent, groceries, bills.

Wants: Netflix, eating out, new shoes.

Goals: Emergency fund, debt payments.

Step 3: Pick a Budget Style

50/30/20 Rule:

50% needs, 30% wants, 20% savings/debt.

Envelope System: Cash in labeled envelopes for each category.

Free Tools:

Apps

Mint, EveryDollar.

Printable budget sheets: Search Pinterest for "simple budget template."

5 Hacks to Save Without Suffering

- "No-Spend" Weekends: Hike, library trips, or board games instead of shopping.
- Meal Prep: Save 200/month by packing lunches (try 5 "budget meal" YouTube videos).
- Slash Subscriptions: Cancel one unused service today (gym? Streaming?).
- Change Jar: Drop spare coins daily—$50/month adds up!
- 24-Hour Rule: Wait a day before buying non-essentials.

Debt Destroyer Plan

Snowball Method: Pay smallest debt first (quick wins = motivation!).

Avalanche Method: Tackle high-interest debt first (save money long-term).

Example:

Credit card: $500 (18% interest).

Student loan: $10,000 (6% interest).

Snowball: Pay your credit card first. Avalanche: Still credit card!

Real-Life Wins

The Green Family:

Challenge: Living paycheck-to-paycheck.

Fix: Cut subscriptions, cooked at home, saved $300/month.

Result: Built a 3-month emergency fund. "We sleep better now!"

Rachel's Debt Freedom:

Challenge: Overwhelming student loans.

Fix: Took freelance gigs, and ate ramen for a year.

Result: Paid off $15k debt. "Freedom tastes better than takeout!"

Martinez Family Vacation:

Challenge: "We'll never afford a trip."

Fix: "No-spend November" + free family fun (park picnics, DIY crafts).

Result: Saved $1,200 for a beach getaway.

Your Action Plan

- Track Spending: Use your phone's notes app for 3 days.
- Slash One Expense: Cancel a subscription or skip Starbucks Friday.
- **Start a 5Jar** or Save5Jar**:Save $5 bills—you'll stash $100 fast!

Need Help?

Free Courses: Khan Academy (personal finance basics).

Community Resources: Local libraries often host free money workshops.

Next Up: Chapter 12 explores Work-Life Balance Without Burnout.

Chapter Twelve

Work-Life Balance Without Burnout

Simple Hacks to Thrive at Work and Home

Work-life balance is the ability to maintain a healthy equilibrium between professional responsibilities and personal life, ensuring that neither one overwhelms the other.

It is essential for overall well-being, as excessive work can lead to burnout, stress, and strained relationships, while too little engagement in meaningful work may cause financial or personal dissatisfaction.

Achieving work-life balance allows individuals to be more productive, focused, and fulfilled in both their careers and personal lives. It also promotes better mental and physical health by reducing stress, improving sleep, and allowing time for self-care, hobbies, and family.

Prioritizing this balance leads to greater happiness, increased motivation, and a more sustainable and satisfying lifestyle.

Why Balance Matters

Constantly juggling work and life? You're not alone. Burnout costs businesses $190 billion yearly (APA), but small changes can protect your peace.

Four Time Management Hacks for Busy Lives

1. The Eisenhower Matrix: Sort Tasks Like a Pro

Urgent + Important: Do these now (e.g., deadlines, crises).

Important + Not Urgent: Schedule these (e.g., family time, long-term goals).

Urgent + Not Important: Delegate (e.g., some emails, meetings).

Not Urgent + Not Important: Delete (e.g., endless scrolling).

Real-Life Win: Sarah, a nurse, used this to cut overtime by 10 hours/week. "I finally have energy for my kids!"

2. Time Blocking: Protect Your Sanity

How: Divide your day into chunks (e.g., 9–11 AM: Work | 3–4 PM: Errands | 7–8 PM: Family).

Pro Tip: Color-code blocks on a free app like Google Calendar.

3. Pomodoro Technique: Work Smarter, Not Harder

25 mins work → 5 mins break (repeat 4x → 30 mins rest).

Free Tool: Use a kitchen timer or Focus Keeper app.

4. The ABCDE Method: Prioritize Like a CEO

A: Critical tasks (do today).

B: Important but can wait (schedule).

C: Nice to do (delegate).

D: Dump or delete.

E: Eliminate (timewasters).

The 80/20 Rule: Focus on What Actually Works

- 20% of efforts create 80% of results.

Example: If a client calls, drive most sales, and cut time on low-impact tasks like lengthy reports.

Real-Life Balance Wins

Mark's Commute Hack:

Challenge: A 2-hour daily drive drained him.

Fix: Switched to audiobooks on leadership + mindfulness.

Result: "I arrive energized, not exhausted."

The Thompson Family's Friday Rule:

Challenge: Weekends felt chaotic.

Fix: "Chore Fridays" freed Saturdays for hikes/picnics.

Result: "We actually enjoy weekends now!"

Emily's Morning Ritual:

Challenge: Overwhelmed by work + parenting.

Fix: Woke up 30 mins early for yoga + coffee in silence.

Result: "I'm calmer, even when chaos hits."

Your Action Plan

- Try One Technique: Start with Pomodoro or Time Blocking today.
- Audit Tasks: Use the Eisenhower Matrix to dump 3 low-priority tasks.
- Family Meeting: Agree on one "protected time" block (e.g., tech-free dinners).

Free Resources

Apps

Trello (task management), Forest (focus timer).

YouTube: Search "10-minute desk stretches."

Next Up: Chapter 13 explores Nature Therapy on a Budget.

Chapter Thirteen

Nature Therapy on a Budget

Find Calm in Green Spaces
No Hiking Required

Nature therapy, also known as ecotherapy or green therapy, is the practice of using nature and outdoor environments to improve mental well-being. It involves activities such as walking in a park, gardening, hiking, or simply spending time in natural settings to reduce stress and promote emotional healing. Exposure to nature has been shown to lower cortisol levels, decrease anxiety, and improve mood by providing a calming and restorative environment. Being in nature also enhances mindfulness, helping individuals feel more present and connected to their surroundings.

Additionally, fresh air, sunlight, and physical activity associated with outdoor experiences contribute to overall health and well-being. Prioritizing time in nature fosters relaxation, boosts creativity, and strengthens resilience, making it a powerful tool for maintaining mental and emotional balance.

Why Nature Heals

Science proves nature is a free therapist:

- 20 minutes in a park cuts stress hormones by 28% (University of Michigan).
- Houseplants boost focus by 15% (NASA Study).

Good news: You don't need a forest—balconies, local parks, or even a single plant work!

Outdoor Hacks for Busy Lives

1. The 5-Minute Green Break:

Step outside. Breathe deeply. Notice three things: a bird, a leaf, the sky.

2. Walk & Talk Meetings:

Ditch the Zoom screen. Discuss projects while strolling a park.

3. Picnic Therapy:

Lunch on a blanket (even in your backyard!). No phone, just sandwiches + sunshine.

4. Tree Meditation:

Lean against a tree. Close your eyes. Listen to leaves rustle for 2 mins.

Family Fun:

- Scavenger Hunts: Kids find a pinecone, a red leaf, something fuzzy.

- Cloud Stories: Lie down, spot shapes in the clouds, and makeup tales.

Indoor Nature Sanctuaries

1. $5 Plant Rescue:

Grab a snake plant or pothos (hard to kill!). It purifies air, lifts mood.

2. DIY Nature Art:

Frame fallen leaves, paint rocks, or arrange twigs in a vase.

3. Sunlight Hack:

Move your desk near a window. Soak up natural light for better focus.

4. Nature Sounds:

Play "forest rain" or "ocean waves" on YouTube during work breaks.

Julia's Transformation

Julia's Garden Recovery:

Challenge: Depression after a divorce.

Fix: Grew tomatoes in pots on her fire escape.

Result: "Watching something grow made me believe I could too."

The Patel Family's Hike Habit:

Challenge: City stress fraying family bonds.

Fix: Sunday hikes in a nearby park.

Result: "We laugh more, argue less—even the teens put phones down!"

Michael's Commute Detour:

Challenge: Panic attacks during subway rides.

Fix: Walked through a park instead.

Result: "Fresh air + trees quieted my mind. I'm 10 mins late but 100% calmer."

Your Action Plan

- Go Micro: Add one plant to your space today (try a $3 succulent!).
- Nature Date: Schedule 15 mins outside this week—no screens allowed.
- Share the Green: Text a friend: "Let's walk and talk instead of coffee?"

Need Help?

Free Apps

AllTrails (find local parks), PlantNet (identify plants).

YouTube: Search "5-minute balcony garden."

Next Up: Chapter 14 - Laughter & Joy on a Budget.

Chapter Fourteen

Laughter & Joy on a Budget

Boost Mental Health with Free, Everyday Delights

Laughter and joy are powerful tools for enhancing mental health, as they help reduce stress, boost mood, and promote overall emotional well-being. Laughter triggers the release of endorphins, the body's natural "feel-good" chemicals, which improve mood and create a sense of happiness. It also lowers cortisol levels, reducing stress and tension in both the mind and body.

Experiencing joy through laughter fosters stronger social connections, strengthens relationships, and provides a natural coping mechanism during difficult times. Additionally, laughter improves cognitive function, increases energy, and even enhances immune system function.

By embracing humor, playfulness, and moments of joy, individuals can cultivate a more positive mindset, build resilience, and improve their overall quality of life.

Why Laughter is Medicine

Science backs it up:

- 10 minutes of laughter cuts stress hormones by 39% (APA).
- Joyful activities boost endorphins (your brain's "feel-good" chemicals) in 5 minutes.

Good news: You don't need a comedy club—joy is hiding in plain sight!

5-Minute Joy Boosters

Quick, free ways to spark laughter and gratitude:

- The "Laughter Log": Jot down one funny moment daily (e.g., your dog's Zoom meeting cameo).
- Silly Selfie Challenge: Snap exaggerated faces with family—worst photo wins!
- Gratitude Scavenger Hunt: Find three things you're grateful for (e.g., morning coffee, a text from a friend).
- Dance Break: Blast a goofy song (try "I Like to Move It") and wiggle like no one's watching.
- Comedy Karaoke: Recite memes or jokes in dramatic voices.

Humor Hacks for Busy Lives

1. Workplace Wins:

Start meetings with a "Happy Headline" (share one positive news story).

Tape a funny meme to your monitor—refresh it weekly.

2. Family Fun:

Joke Jar: Fill a jar with dad jokes. Pull one at dinner, e.g., Why don't skeletons fight? They don't have the guts!

Meme Exchange: Create a family group chat for sharing funny pet/kid videos.

3. Solo Smiles:

Watch one stand-up clip on YouTube (try Iliza Shlesinger or Trevor Noah).

Follow @doggosdoingthings on Instagram for instant joy.

Gratitude Without the Guilt

No journals required—try these:

Grocery Line Game: Mentally list three things you're grateful for while waiting.

Thank-You Texts: Send one unexpected "TY for being awesome" message daily.

Gratitude Wall: Post sticky notes on the fridge, "Thankful for pizza Fridays!"

Pro Tip: Pair gratitude with laughter—write a funny reason you're thankful for Wi-Fi.

Real-Life Application

Maria's Laughter Yoga:

Challenge: Depression made daily tasks exhausting.

Fix: Joined free laughter yoga at the community center.

Result: "Fake laughs turned real. I forgot to be sad for a while."

The Smith Family's Game Night:

Challenge: Work/school stress caused constant bickering.

Fix: Weekly "Charades Fail Night" (think interpretive dance for "toaster").

Result: "We laugh so hard; stress doesn't stand a chance."

Tom's Stand-Up Therapy:

Challenge: Social anxiety kept him isolated.

Fix: Told jokes at an open mic night.

Result: "Mess-ups made people laugh with me, not at me. Game-changer!"

Your Action Plan

- Try One Booster: Dance break or joke jar—pick your joy poison.
- Text a Smile: Send a meme to someone who's stressed.
- Celebrate Small Wins: High-five yourself after each laugh.

Need Help?

Free Apps

Laughscape (curated comedy clips), Happyfeed (gratitude journal).

YouTube: Search "5-minute laughter yoga."

Next Up: Chapter 15 - Family Dynamics on a Budget.

Chapter Fifteen

Family Dynamics on a Budget

Strengthen Bonds, Build Resilience, and Thrive Together

Family dynamics refer to the patterns of interactions, relationships, and roles within a family unit that shape how members communicate and support one another. These dynamics play a crucial role in mental health, as a healthy family environment provides emotional security, encouragement, and a sense of belonging.

Positive family relationships foster self-esteem, resilience, and healthy coping mechanisms, helping individuals navigate life's challenges with confidence.

On the other hand, dysfunctional family dynamics—such as conflict, lack of communication, or emotional neglect—can contribute to stress, anxiety, and long-term emotional struggles.

Understanding and improving family dynamics through open communication, respect, and support can significantly enhance mental well-being, creating a foundation for strong, healthy relationships both within and outside the family.

Why Family Connection Matters

Families are your first support system.

Science shows strong family bonds:

- Reduce anxiety by 34% (APA).
- Boost kids' academic success by 40% (*Journal of Family Psychology*).

Good news: Deepening connections doesn't cost a dime—just intention and time.

5-Minute Communication Hacks

Transform everyday moments into meaningful connections:

- The "Device-Free Dinner" Rule: No phones at meals. Ask: "What made you laugh today?"
- Active Listening Game: Take turns sharing a story. The listener repeats back three key points.
- Gratitude Tag: At bedtime, tag a family member with "I'm grateful you…"
- Emotion Charades: Act out feelings (happy, frustrated) and guess them—kids love this!
- The "I Feel" Challenge: Replace "You always…" with "I feel [emotion] when…"

Build Your Family Support Toolkit

1. Weekly Check-Ins (No Therapy Couch Needed)

When: Sunday nights over popcorn.

Agenda:

Highs & Lows: Each shares one win and one struggle.

Plan Fun: Brainstorm a free activity (e.g., backyard campout).

Solve It: Pick one small issue to tackle together (e.g., chore fairness).

2. Conflict Resolution on a Budget

Step 1: Call a "Pause" when tensions rise. Take 5 mins alone to breathe.

Step 2: Use the "Feelings First" Script:

"I feel [emotion] when [action]. Can we try [solution]?"

Example: "I feel overwhelmed when dishes pile up. Can we rotate cleanup duty?"

3. Tech-Free Zones

Where: Bedrooms + dining area.

Why: Screens drain connection. Replace with a "Joke Board" (post funny notes).

Real-Life Family Wins

The Garcia Family's Anxiety Breakthrough:

Challenge: Daughter Mia's anxiety isolated her.

Fix: Weekly "Highs & Lows" chats over pancake breakfasts.

Result: "Mia shares more, and we laugh harder. Her panic attacks dropped!"

The Robinsons' Healing Creative Nights:

Challenge: Grief after losing a parent.

Fix: Friday art nights such as drawing memories, making music playlists.

Result: "We cry, but we also laugh. It's how we heal together."

The Smiths' Tech Detox:

Challenge: Phones replaced family time.

Fix: "Screen-Free Sundays" with hikes and board games.

Result: "Our kids actually talk to us now—wild, right?"

Your Action Plan

- Start Small: Try one 5-minute hack this week (e.g., Gratitude Tag).
- Schedule a Check-In: 15 mins, no prep needed. Ask: "How can I support you this week?"
- Celebrate Wins: High-five when someone uses an "I Feel" statement.

Free Resources

Apps

Cozi (family calendar), Happy Family (free parenting courses).

YouTube: Search "5-minute family yoga."

Next Up: Chapter 16 explores Volunteerism on a Budget.

Chapter Sixteen

Volunteerism on a Budget

Boost Your Mood by Helping Others No Time or Money Needed

Volunteering is a rewarding experience that benefits both the individual and the community. It provides a sense of purpose and fulfillment, allowing people to contribute their time and skills to meaningful causes. Volunteering can also help build strong social connections, reducing feelings of isolation while fostering a sense of belonging. Additionally, it offers opportunities for personal and professional growth by enhancing skills, gaining experience, and even opening doors to new career paths. On a mental and emotional level, giving back can boost self-esteem and overall well-being, as acts of kindness and service have been linked to increased happiness. Ultimately, volunteering not only improves the lives of those in need but also enriches the lives of those who choose to serve.

Why Volunteering Heals

- Helping others isn't just kind—it's science-backed therapy:

- Reduces stress: 94% of volunteers report improved mood (APA).
- Fights loneliness: Connecting with others cuts isolation.
- Builds purpose: Feeling useful boosts self-worth.
- Good news: You don't need hours or cash. Even small acts make a difference.

Find Local Opportunities in 3 Steps

Match Skills to Needs:

Love cooking? ➜ Soup kitchens.

Good with kids? ➜ Tutor at libraries.

Hands-on? ➜ Park clean-ups or animal shelters.

Check These Spots:

Community boards: Grocery stores, libraries.

Schools: Help with events or mentorship programs.

Places of worship: Food drives, visiting seniors.

Start Small:

Commit to 1–2 hours a month. Even picking up litter counts!

Virtual Volunteering: Help from Home

No car? No problem! Try these free, flexible options:

Skill-Based:

- Catchafire: Use your job skills (design, writing) for nonprofits.

- UN Volunteers: Translate documents or mentor globally.

Micro-Actions

- Write letters to isolated seniors via Letters Against Isolation.
- Review resumes for job seekers on Upchieve.

Advocacy

- Share mental health resources on social media.
- Sign online petitions (e.g., mental health funding).

Pro Tip: Set a weekly 30-minute "virtual volunteering" block.

Real-Life Volunteer Wins

Emily's Baking Therapy:

Challenge: Job loss triggered anxiety.

Fix: Baked treats for a shelter.

Result: "Seeing smiles over my cookies gave me purpose again."

The Patel Family Garden:

Challenge: Felt disconnected from neighbors.

Fix: Started a free community veggie patch.

Result: "We grow food and friendships. Our kids love it!"

Tom's Hospital Healing:

Challenge: PTSD from a car accident.

Fix: Volunteered at a hospital, comforting families.

Result: "Listening to others' stories helped me process my pain."

Your Action Plan

Pick One Tiny Task:

- Donate old books to a library.
- Write a 5-star review for a local nonprofit's Google page.
- Skill Swap: Offer 30 mins of your expertise (e.g., resume help) online.
- Family Challenge: Volunteer together once a month (e.g., park cleanup).

Free Tools

Ctrl-Alt-CALM App.

VolunteerMatch: Filters opportunities by location/cause.

DoSomething.org: Quick, youth-friendly campaigns.

Next Up: Chapter 17 - Healing Through Books.

Chapter Seventeen

Healing Through Books

How Reading Can Boost Mental Health, No Cost Required

Healing through reading books, often referred to as bibliotherapy, can be incredibly beneficial for mental, emotional, and even physical well-being. Books offer a safe escape, allowing readers to immerse themselves in different worlds, perspectives, and experiences that can provide comfort and reassurance.

Reading can help reduce stress, improve focus, and promote relaxation, making it an effective coping mechanism during difficult times. Additionally, books can provide wisdom, guidance, and inspiration, helping individuals process emotions, gain new insights, and find solutions to personal struggles. Whether through fiction, self-help, or memoirs, reading can foster healing by offering validation, emotional release, and a renewed sense of hope.

Why Books Heal

- Books are silent therapists.

- Science shows reading: Reduces stress by 68% (University of Sussex).
- Builds empathy and emotional resilience.

Good news: You don't need a degree, just a library card or online subscription!

Find Your Healing Book

1. Self-Help Guides:

Try: The Anxiety Toolkit or Atomic Habits.

Why: Practical steps to tackle stress, sleep, or confidence.

2. Memoirs:

Try: Educated (Tara Westover) or Reasons to Stay Alive (Matt Haig).

Why: Real stories remind you you're not alone.

3. Fiction:

Try: The Alchemist (adventure) or Eleanor Oliphant Is Completely Fine (loneliness).

Why: Stories help process emotions safely.

4. Graphic Novels:

Try: Persepolis (resilience) or Hey, Kiddo (family struggles).

Why: Visual storytelling for tough topics.

Pro Tip: Ask librarians for recommendations—they're free book therapists!

Read Without Stress

Audiobooks: Listen while walking or cooking (try Libby app for free library loans).

15-Minute Rule: Read one chapter daily —no pressure to finish. These days, there are book summaries that can be completed within 15 minutes.

Trigger Warning: Skip books that upset you. It's OK to quit!

Family Hack: Read aloud together—kids' books like *The Boy, the Mole, the Fox* and *the Horse* spark deep talks.

Join a Book Club (Yes, Really!)

Free Options

Local libraries: Often host clubs (in-person or online).

Goodreads: Virtual groups for every genre.

Perks: Meet friends, gain perspectives, laugh/cry together.

Example: Sarah's Online Club: Busy moms chat books at midnight—no pants required!

Real-Life Wins

John's Burnout Breakthrough:

Challenge: Crushed by corporate stress.

Fix: Read *Wherever You Go, There You Are* (mindfulness).

Result: "I meditate daily now. My team says I'm calmer!"

Emily's Confidence Boost:

Challenge: Too shy to speak in class.

Fix: Joined a YA book club at school.

Result: "Discussing characters gave me the courage to raise my hand!"

Mark & Lisa's Marriage Reset:

Challenge: Constant arguments.

Fix: Read *The 5 Love Languages* together.

Result: "We 'argue' over book plots now, not chores!"

Your Action Plan

- Grab One Book: Visit the library or download a free eBook.
- Try Audiobooks: Listen to a memoir during your commute.
- Text a Friend: "Let's read the same book this month!"

Free Tools

Project Gutenberg: 60,000+ free classic eBooks.

Libby: Borrow library audiobooks instantly.

Next Up: Chapter 18 reveals Music as Mental Medicine.

Chapter Eighteen

Music as Mental Medicine

Harness Sound for Calm, Joy, and Connection

No Concert Tickets Needed

Music therapy is a powerful tool that promotes healing and well-being by using music to address physical, emotional, cognitive, and social needs. It has been shown to reduce stress, anxiety, and depression while enhancing mood and overall mental health.

Through rhythm, melody, and harmony, music therapy can help individuals express emotions that may be difficult to verbalize, making it especially beneficial for those dealing with trauma, neurological disorders, or communication challenges. It can also aid in pain management, improve cognitive function, and support physical rehabilitation by stimulating movement and coordination.

Whether through listening, playing instruments, singing, or composing, music therapy provides a therapeutic and uplifting experience that fosters connection, relaxation, and inner healing.

Why Music Works?

Science sings its praises:

- Reduces anxiety by 65% (University of Nevada).
- Boosts dopamine (the "feel-good" chemical) in 15 minutes.
- Strengthens bonds when shared with others.

Good news: Your phone + free apps = instant mood lifter.

Create Mood-Boosting Playlists

1. Stress-Buster Mix:

Songs: Acoustic covers, classical piano, nature sounds.

Try: Spotify's "Peaceful Piano" or YouTube "Calm Vibes."

2. Energy Boost Playlist:

Songs: Upbeat pop, disco classics, drum-heavy tracks.

Pro Tip: Add your go-to gym jams or childhood favorites.

3. Sadness Soothers:

Songs: Ballads with hopeful lyrics, e.g., "Here Comes the Sun."

Avoid: Songs that spiral you deeper—curate with care!

4. Family Joy List:

Songs: Kid-friendly bops (*Disney, Encanto*), throwback hits.

Activity: Dance breaks while cooking or cleaning!

Free Tools

Spotify: Search "mood" playlists (e.g., "Anxiety Relief").

YouTube: Stream "Lofi beats" for focus or relaxation.

Free Musical Activities

1. Kitchen Concerts:

Grab pots, spoons, or a hairbrush mic. Belt out classics!

2. Community Choirs:

Check libraries or churches for free singing groups.

3. Nature Soundwalks:

Listen to birds, rustling leaves, or street musicians.

4. Karaoke Nights:

Use YouTube karaoke tracks + a flashlight "stage."

5. Music Therapy Lite:

DIY: Hum, whistle, or drum rhythms when stressed.

Real-Life Wins

Sarah's Playlist Power:

Challenge: Panic attacks during commutes.

Fix: Made a "Calm Commute" mix with ocean sounds + piano.

Result: "I arrive relaxed, not rattled."

The Johnson Family Band:

Challenge: Sibling squabbles every night.

Fix: Friday "jam sessions" with ukulele + tambourine.

Result: "We fight less and laugh more—even the teens join!"

Tom's Drumming Recovery:

Challenge: Isolation after a heart attack.

Fix: Joined a free community drum circle.

Result: "The rhythm helped my heart—and my mood."

Your Action Plan

- Build One Playlist: Pick a mood (calm, joy, focus) and curate five songs.
- Sing in the Shower: Bonus points for dramatic flair!
- Text a Song: Share a track that lifts you with someone who needs it.

Need Help?

Free Apps

SoundCloud (indie mixes), Insight Timer (healing music).

Local Gems: Parks often host free summer concerts.

Next Up: Chapter 19 explores Affirmations on a Budget.

Chapter Nineteen

Affirmations on a Budget

Boost Confidence & Crush Negativity
Zero Cost Required

Affirmations are positive statements that help reframe negative thoughts and reinforce self-belief, confidence, and motivation. They are important because they shape our mindset, influence our emotions, and ultimately impact our actions.

By regularly repeating affirmations, individuals can train their minds to focus on strengths, goals, and possibilities rather than doubts and limitations. Research suggests that affirmations can reduce stress, boost self-esteem, and promote a more optimistic outlook on life.

They can also help rewire negative thought patterns, fostering a sense of empowerment and resilience. Whether used for self-improvement, overcoming challenges, or cultivating gratitude, affirmations serve as a powerful tool for personal growth and mental well-being.

Why Affirmations Work

Science says positive self-talk:

- Reduces stress by 31% (APA).
- Boosts self-esteem in just 2 weeks (*Journal of Positive Psychology*).

Rewires your brain to focus on strengths, not flaws.

Good news: You don't need a therapist, just a mirror and 5 minutes!

Build Your Daily Affirmation Routine

Step 1: Start Small

Pick 1–3 phrases like "I am enough" or "I handle challenges with calm."

Step 2: Morning Momentum

Say them aloud while brushing your teeth or sipping coffee.

Pro Tip: Stick notes on your bathroom mirror or fridge.

Step 3: Family Affirmation Time

At dinner, share one positive phrase, "We support each other."

Kids love: "I am brave!" or "Today will be awesome!"

Step 4: Track Progress

Use a free app like Grateful or a $1 notebook to jot wins.

Vision Boards Made Simple

Visualize goals without Pinterest-perfect pressure:

Grab Supplies: Old magazines, scissors, glue, poster board.

Cut & Paste:

Images: Dream job, travel spots, happy family moments.

Words: "Confidence," "Joy," "Adventure."

Add Affirmations: Write "I am capable" or "Success is mine."

Display & Reflect: Hang where you'll see it daily (closet door, workspace).

Free Digital Option: Use Canva to create a vision board on your phone.

Real-Life Application

Mia's Affirmation Jar:

Challenge: Self-doubt at work.

Fix: Wrote "I am skilled and valued" on slips of paper.

Result: "Reading one each morning silenced my inner critic."

The Lopez Family Dinner Ritual:

Challenge: Negative talk after school/work.

Fix: Shared affirmations like "We celebrate small wins."

Result: "Dinner became our favorite mood booster!"

Aisha's Mirror Magic:

Challenge: Morning anxiety.

Fix: Recited "I am calm and capable" while brushing hair.

Result: "I walk into meetings feeling unstoppable."

Your Action Plan

- Write One Affirmation Now: "I choose joy today."
- Family Challenge: Create a shared vision board this weekend.
- Text a Friend: Share your favorite affirmation—inspire each other!

Free Tools

ThinkUp: Record affirmations in your voice.

Pinterest: Search "vision board ideas" for instant inspiration.

Next Up: Chapter 20 - Spiritual Healing and Mental Health.

Chapter Twenty

Spiritual Healing and Mental Health

Faith-Based Tools for Peace, Strength, and Renewed Purpose

Faith and spiritual healing are deeply interconnected, as faith provides a foundation for hope, resilience, and emotional well-being during times of struggle. Believing in a higher power or a greater purpose can offer comfort and strength, helping individuals navigate challenges with a sense of peace and trust.

Spiritual healing, which often involves prayer, meditation, or mindfulness, allows people to release stress, find clarity, and cultivate inner harmony.

Many believe that faith can facilitate physical healing by reducing anxiety and promoting a positive mindset, which can contribute to overall well-being. Whether through religious devotion, spiritual practices, or a personal belief system, faith nurtures the soul, fosters healing, and provides a sense of connection to something greater than oneself.

Why Faith Matters for Mental Health

Faith has been shown to reduce stress and improve mental resilience significantly. Studies indicate that prayer and meditation lower cortisol levels, the stress hormone, by 20% (APA, 2023).

Nurturing one's spiritual well-being, whether through prayer, reflection, or acts of service, can play a crucial role in maintaining mental balance.

Feeling overwhelmed? You're not alone. Millions find hope and calm through spiritual practices—no expensive therapy or apps needed. Faith in Jesus offers free, timeless tools to ease anxiety, depression, and burnout.

Quick Takeaway: prayer, scripture, and community can anchor you during life's storms.

How Faith Fuels Resilience

1. Faith Covers Every Part of Your Life

God cares about all of you—mind, body, and soul.

Basis: *3 John 2* (AMP) says, "I pray that you may prosper in every way…"

Science: Studies show prayer lowers stress hormones like cortisol.

Try This Now:

- Morning: Start your day with 5 minutes of gratitude prayer.
- Night: Read one Bible verse (e.g., Matthew 11:28-30) before bed.

4 Free, Fast Faith Hacks

Pray Anywhere, Anytime

Stuck in traffic? Whisper, "God, I need Your peace."

Bonus: Writing prayers in a notes app counts, too!

Scripture Snacks

Overwhelmed? Memorize *Isaiah 41:10*: "Fear not, I am with you…"

Gratitude Jar

Family Hack: Have everyone drop a "thankful note to God" in a jar weekly. Read them aloud on Sundays.

2-Minute Devotionals

Use free apps like YouVersion for quick daily readings.

Real-Life Victory: Maria's Story

Maria, 35, lost her job and sank into depression. After joining a church group, she:

Prayed daily: "God, help me trust Your plan."

Joined a Bible study: Found friends who encouraged her.

Result: Landed a new job and rebuilt her confidence.

Your Turn: What's one small step you can take this week?

Build a Faith Routine That Fits Your Life

For Busy Schedules:

- Commute Prayer: Talk to God during your drive or subway ride.
- Scripture Post-Its: Stick verses on your fridge, desk, or mirror.

For Families:

- Dinnertime Devotionals: Discuss a Bible story (e.g., Elijah's hope in hard times).
- Serve Together: Volunteer at a food bank—teaches kids compassion and gratitude.

God's Promises = Your Anxiety Antidote

When Fear Strikes:

Psalm 23:4: "I will fear no evil, for You are with me."

Isaiah 41:10: "I will strengthen you and help you."

Action Step: Write these on your phone's lock screen. Repeat them aloud when stress hits.

Faith Communities: Your Support Squad

Why It Works:

- Shared stories = less loneliness.
- Prayer groups = instant hope boost.
- Budget-Friendly Options:
- Free Church Groups: Many offer support for anxiety, grief, or parenting.
- Online Communities: Facebook groups like "Faith Over Fear" (24/7 encouragement).

Quick FAQ

Q: "I'm not religious. Can this help me?"
A: Start small! Try a gratitude jar, or nature walks to reflect. Spiritual peace isn't one-size-fits-all.

Q: "How do I find time?"

A: Swap 5 minutes of social media scrolling for a devotional.

Your Next Step

Today: Pick one tip above (e.g., 5-minute prayer). This Week: Text a friend: "Want to try a faith hack with me?"

Bottom Line: You don't need a perfect prayer life or hours of free time. Start small, lean on God's promises, and watch hope grow.

"With God, all things are possible." – *Matthew 19:26*

Next up: Chapter Twenty-one explores Long-term Planning for Mental Resilience.

Chapter Twenty-One

Long-Term Planning for Mental Resilience

Sustain Your Progress with Values, Driven Habits & Flexible Strategies

Mental resilience is the ability to adapt, recover, and thrive in the face of stress, adversity, or challenges. It's what helps people bounce back from difficulties, maintain emotional balance, and keep moving forward despite setbacks.

Key aspects of mental resilience include:

- **Emotional regulation** – Managing stress, fear, and frustration effectively.
- **Optimism** – Maintaining a positive yet realistic outlook.
- **Self-awareness** – Understanding personal strengths, weaknesses, and triggers.
- **Problem-solving skills** – Finding solutions instead of being overwhelmed by problems.
- **Social support** – Seeking help and maintaining strong relationships.

- **Adaptability** – Adjusting to change without losing focus or motivation.

It's not about avoiding hardship but learning to navigate it with strength and confidence. Would you like tips on building mental resilience?

Long-term planning for mental resilience involves developing habits and strategies that strengthen emotional endurance and adaptability over time. It includes setting realistic goals, cultivating a growth mindset, and building a strong support system to navigate life's challenges with confidence.

Prioritizing self-care, practicing mindfulness, and engaging in activities that promote emotional well-being can enhance one's ability to cope with stress and adversity.

Developing problem-solving skills and embracing change with a proactive mindset also contribute to long-term resilience. Additionally, seeking therapy or counseling when needed ensures ongoing mental health maintenance. By consistently nurturing mental strength, individuals can build the resilience necessary to thrive in both personal and professional aspects of life.

Why Long-Term Resilience Matters

Life's ups and downs can derail even the best intentions. A values-driven plan acts like a compass, guiding you through challenges without burnout or overwhelm.

Quick Takeaway: Align your mental health goals with what matters most—family, creativity, connection—to stay motivated for the long haul.

Step 1: Build Your Mental Health Compass

What Fuels You?

Family: Schedule weekly game nights or walks.

Career: Block "no-work zones" (e.g., evenings after 7 PM).

Creativity: Dedicate 15 minutes daily to a hobby (drawing, cooking, etc.).

Social Connections: Host a monthly potluck or join a free community group.

Action Tip: Write your top value on a sticky note and post it where you'll see it daily, e.g., on the fridge or your laptop.

Step 2: Set S-M-A-R-T Goals (Free & Easy!)

Transform vague intentions into clear wins:

Specific: "Journal for 10 minutes nightly to unwind."

Measurable: "Track mood changes weekly using a free app like Daylio."

Achievable: "Walk 3x/week—no marathon needed!"

Relevant: "Join a book club to meet like-minded people."

Time-Bound: "Read one stress-management article every Sunday."

For Families: Turn goal setting into a game—reward milestones with a picnic or movie night!

Step 3: Adapt Like a Pro

Life changes? So can your plan!

Your Mental Health GPS:

Weekly Check-In: Ask: "Does this goal still fit my life?"

Pivot, Don't Quit: Too busy for hour-long workouts? Try 10-minute YouTube yoga (e.g., Yoga With Adriene).

Celebrate Tiny Wins: Finished a 5-minute meditation? Do a victory dance!

Real-Life Resilience Wins

Rachel's Routine: Stressed and burned out, she added 10-minute journaling and lunchtime walks. Result: Better focus, less anxiety.

The Johnsons' Family Meetings: Monthly check-ins + shared chores = stronger bonds.

Juan's Community Boost: Volunteering at a food bank gave him purpose—and new friends.

Your Turn: What's one small habit you can start this week?

Troubleshooting Guide: Beat Common Roadblocks

"No Time!"

Fix It Fast: Swap 15 minutes of scrolling for a walk or deep-breathing exercise.

Procrastination

Fix It Fast: Use the "2-Minute Rule"—start a tiny task (e.g., open your journal). Momentum builds!

Negative Self-Talk

Fix It Fast: Write a mantra: "I am enough. Progress > perfection."

Overwhelm

Fix It Fast: Pick one free app (e.g., Insight Timer for meditation) and stick with it for 7 days.

Loneliness

Fix It Fast: Text a friend: "Want to try a 5-minute mindfulness challenge with me?"

Budget-Friendly Resilience Boosters

Free Apps

Smiling Mind (meditation), Finch (self-care goals).

Community Resources

Library workshops, park clean-up groups.

DIY Tools: Gratitude jar ($0—use a mason jar and scrap paper).

Next Steps

Today: Write one S-M-A-R-T goal, e.g., "Walk 10 minutes after dinner, 3x/week."

This Month: Host a 15-minute family check-in to share wins and struggles.

Bottom Line: Resilience isn't about never falling—it's about learning to bounce back stronger. Start small, stay flexible, and let your values lead the way.

"You don't have to see the whole staircase. Just take the first step." – Martin Luther King Jr.

Up Next: Chapter 22 – Conclusion.

Chapter Twenty-Two

Conclusion

Your Journey to Lifelong Mental Wellness Starts Now

Your journey to lifelong mental wellness starts now, and it begins with intentional choices that prioritize your emotional and psychological well-being. Cultivating a healthy mindset involves self-awareness, self-care, and the willingness to embrace growth and change. By incorporating mindfulness, positive affirmations, and stress-management techniques into your daily routine, you create a strong foundation for resilience and inner peace.

Building supportive relationships, setting personal boundaries, and seeking professional guidance when needed are also key steps toward maintaining long-term mental health.

Every step you take—no matter how small—brings you closer to a balanced, fulfilling life. Start today, and commit to nurturing your mind, body, and spirit for a lifetime of wellness and happiness.

Reflect & Celebrate: How Far You've Come

Take a deep breath. You've just equipped yourself with 21 chapters of practical, budget-friendly tools to tackle anxiety, burnout, and more. Before rushing ahead, ask yourself:

What's one strategy that surprised you? Example: "5-minute meditation actually works!"

When did you feel most empowered? Example: "Journaling helped me spot stress triggers."

What small win can you celebrate today? Example: "I prioritized sleep this week!"

Write your answers here:

_____

_____

_____

_____

_____

_____

Your Next Steps: Brass-Tacks Action Plan

Small Steps, Big Changes. Progress isn't about perfection; it's about tiny, consistent steps that add up overtime. Whether you start with a 5-minute breathing exercise, a short gratitude journal entry, or a screen-free bedtime routine, every step counts. Mental wellness is a journey— one that you don't have to take alone. You've got this!

Here's How To Keep Momentum

1. Pick Your Top 3 Strategies

From this book, choose three hacks to focus on this month. Examples:

Family: Weekly "no-screen" dinners.

Solo: 5-minute morning gratitude journaling.

Budget: Free meditation apps like Insight Timer.

2. Build Your Support Squad

Text a friend: "Want to try a mental health hack together?"

Join a free group: Search Facebook for "Anxiety Support Circle" or Meetup for local wellness events.

3. Schedule Monthly Check-Ins

Set a calendar reminder to ask:

"What's working?" (Keep doing it!)

"What needs tweaking?" (Adjust without guilt!)

Mental Health = A Garden, Not a Quick Fix

Think of your mind like a plant:

- Water it daily: 10 minutes of mindfulness, walks, or laughter.
- Prune the weeds: Limit toxic social media or negative self-talk.
- Adjust with the seasons: Swap summer outdoor yoga for winter cozy reading.

Free Printable: Grab a "Mental Health Garden Tracker" to map your growth!

When Life Throws Curveballs

Stressed about slipping up? Remember:

Progress > Perfection: Missed meditation? Try again tomorrow.

Flexibility = Strength: Swap a 30-minute workout for a 5-minute dance break.

Ask for Help: Free hotlines (e.g., 988 Crisis Lifeline) are there for you.

Real-Life Victory: Sarah's Story

Sarah, a single mom, felt overwhelmed until she:

She used Chapter 5's 5-Minute Breathwork during her commute.

Started a family gratitude jar (Chapter 12).

Joined a free local walking group (Chapter 18). Result: "I'm calmer, and my kids love our new routines!"

Your Turn: What's your first tiny step?

Quick Resilience Checklist

Before closing this book, do these now:

- Text yourself: "I'm worth the effort." Save it as your lock screen.
- Write one goal: "This week, I'll try _____." Tape it to your bathroom mirror.

- Bookmark your favorite chapter for easy re-reading.

Keep Growing: Free Resources

Apps

Ctrl-Alt-CALM.

Finch (self-care pet), Daylio (mood tracking).

Podcasts: The Happiness Lab (science-backed joy tips).

Books: Atomic Habits (tiny changes = big results).

Final Challenge: 30 Days to Stronger Mental Health

Day 1: Hydrate before coffee.

Day 15: Compliment a stranger.

Day 30: Write a "proud moment" letter to yourself.

You've Got This! Every effort counts—even reading this book. Keep it handy, revisit chapters when needed, and remember that small steps create lasting change.

"You are braver than you believe, stronger than you seem, and smarter than you think." —A.A. Milne

Thank you for letting me join your journey.

Now go thrive!

The End.

But Really, It's Just the Beginning!

About the Author

Abiodun Adesina's career spans four decades. He's worked with national and global organizations and is now the founder of 3pplea Holdings.

Six decades of life have taught Abiodun about work-life balance challenges. A family man for about three decades, he's learned a lot about building strong relationships.

Abiodun promotes mental health. In addition to being an entrepreneur and a family man, he's also a mentor and a counselor. He helps people find peace and purpose in their lives.

Abiodun shows that it's possible to achieve success and mental wellness together. By taking care of your mental health, you can have better relationships, do better at work, feel great overall, and live out your purpose.

Abiodun A. Adesina

Dear Reader,

Thank you from the bottom of my heart for reading this book. I hope it has inspired, uplifted, or resonated with you in a meaningful way. Writing this book was a journey, and knowing that you have joined me on it means more than words can express.

Your support as a reader is truly invaluable. If you enjoyed this book, I would be incredibly grateful if you could take a moment to leave an honest review on **Amazon and/or Goodreads**. Your feedback not only helps other readers discover this book but also allows me to continue creating meaningful content for you.

Every review—big or small—makes a difference, and I deeply appreciate your time and effort in sharing your thoughts. Thank you again for being part of this journey. I look forward to connecting with you through future books!

With gratitude,

Abiodun A. Adesina

Appendix

This section includes all free tools, trackers, and bonus materials referenced in the chapters.

Free Apps & Tools

Ctrl-Alt-CALM (Chapter 4): Free and Premium versions available.

Moodfit (Chapter 2): Mood-tracking app.

Habitica (Chapter 3): Gamified habit-building app.

Libby (Chapter 17): Free library audiobooks.

Meetup (Chapter 10): Find local free events.

YouVersion (Chapter 20): Free Bible devotionals.

DIY Guides

Vision Board Kit (Chapter 19): Use old magazines, glue, and cardboard.

Gratitude Jar (Chapter 14): Mason jar + scrap paper.

Kid Calm-Down Jar (Chapter 8): Water + glitter in a sealed container.

References

American Psychological Association (APA). (2023). Stress in America™ Survey.

World Health Organization (WHO). (2023). *Depression and Other Common Mental Disorders.*

University of Michigan. (2021). *Nature's Impact on Stress Reduction.*

National Institute of Mental Health (NIMH). (2022). *Sleep and Mental Health.*

Harvard Study on Adult Development. (2019). *Social Connections and Longevity.*

Khan Academy. (2023). *Personal Finance Basics.*

Mint. (2023). *Budgeting Tools and Resources.*

University of Nevada. (2020). *Music Therapy and Anxiety Reduction.*

NASA Clean Air Study. (1989). *Houseplants and Air Quality.*

Journal of Family Psychology. (2021). *Family Bonds and Academic Success.*

Index

80/20 Rule, 54
ABCDE Method, 54
Affirmations, 82
anxiety, 1, 3, 4, 6, 7, 8, 9, 11, 16, 20, 21, 25, 29, 34, 39, 63, 66, 67, 71, 78, 83, 86, 88, 92, 96
Avalanche Method, 49
Boost Mental Health, 8, 60, 73
Brain Foods, 25
Budget, 48
burnout, 1, 4, 13, 86, 91, 96
Communication Hacks, 66
Community, 44
Conflict Resolution, 67
Connection, 66
creative activities, 31
Creativity, 29, 31, 91
Debt, 49
depression, 3, 4, 8, 20, 34, 44, 86, 87
Detox, 40
endorphins, 20, 29, 61
Envelope System, 48
exercise, 9, 20, 44, 93, 96
Faith, 86

Gratitude, 62
Gratitude Wall, 62
Group Activities, 44
Habit Tracking, 13
Home Workouts, 20
Humor Hacks, 61
Insomnia, 35
Invisible Backpack, 2
Journaling, 30
Joy Boosters, 61
Laughter, 61
Libby, 76
Loneliness and isolation, 8
mental health, 3, 5, 7, 1, 2, 3, 4, 5, 6, 8, 9, 27, 40, 71, 91, 97, 100
Mindfulness, 16
Money Stress, 48
nature, 57
Pomodoro Technique, 53
Project Gutenberg, 76
reading, 74
Resilience, 91
Rituals, 12
Routines, 10
sleep, 3, 20, 22, 34, 35, 37, 39, 50, 74, 96

Social media, 40
Support Squad, 44
Tech Trap, 38
Tech-Free Zones, 39, 67
Teen Tech Curfew, 36
The Domino Effect, 3
The Eisenhower Matrix, 53

Theme Nights, 26
Time Blocking, 53
Time Management, 53
Vision Board, 29, 102
Volunteering, 69
White Noise, 34

Ctrl-Alt-CALM

www.ingramcontent.com/pod-product-compliance
Lightning Source LLC
Chambersburg PA
CBHW072022060426
42449CB00033B/1655